NATIVE NATIONS OF NORTH AMERICA

Life in a PUEBLO

22245

Amanda Bishop & Bobbie Kalman

Crabtree Publishing Company

www.crabtreebooks.com

Life in a PUEBLO

Created by Bobbie Kalman

Dedicated by Amanda Bishop
For Dixie—thanks for the memories

Editor-in-Chief
Bobbie Kalman

Writing team
Amanda Bishop
Bobbie Kalman
Rebecca Sjonger

Editorial director
Niki Walker

Editor
Kathryn Smithyman

Art director
Robert MacGregor

Design
Margaret Amy Reiach

Production coordinator
Heather Fitzpatrick

Photo research
Laura Hysert
Jaimie Nathan

Consultants

John D. Gates, J.D. Lecturer, University of New Mexico Native American Studies
  Department. Enrolled member of the Cheyenne River Sioux Tribe, Eagle Butte, SD.
Rebecca S. Hernandez, Ph.D., Director of Curatorial Affairs, Indian Pueblo Cultural
  Center, Albuquerque, New Mexico

Photographs and reproductions

Circa:Art/Getty Images: front cover, pages 1, 4 (top), 6, 13, 24, 27 (top)
Courtesy of the Eiteljorg Museum of American Indians and Western Art: *Wild
  Plum Blossoms*, Joseph Henry Sharp (image trimmed), 10; *Legend of Montezuma*,
  Eanger Irving Couse, 12; *Deer Hunter's Camp*, Bert Geer Phillips (image trimmed), 19
The Greenwich Workshop, Inc. Shelton, CT: © Tom Lovell: *Pecos Pueblo, About 1500*
  (detail), pages 28-29
Nativestock.com: page 23
Pecos National Historical Park, © Roy Andersen: page 31
© James P. Rowan: page 27 (bottom)
Smithsonian American Art Museum, Washington, DC / Art Resource, NY:
  pages 14, 15, 20, 21, 30
Stark Museum of Art, Orange, Texas: Eanger Irving Couse, *The Pinion Basket*,
  back cover, 22; J. H. Sharp, *Hunting Song*, 7; Bert Geer Phillips, *Spectators at
  Winter Ceremonial, Taos Pueblo*, 8; Oscar E. Berninghaus, *Racers at the Pueblo*, 11;
  Bettina Steinke, *Santa Clara Fiesta Day Dance*, 26
All other images by Digital Stock

Illustrations

Barbara Bedell: pages 16 (bottom), 17 (tools), 18 (except cactus and background),
  19, 21 (top), 25
Katherine Kantor: page 17 (corn field)
Margaret Amy Reiach: border, back cover (hide skin), pages 16 (top), 22,
  23 (left and right)
Bonna Rouse: background (pages 1, 7, 12, 18, 21, 27), pages 9, 17 (corn stalks),
  18 (cactus), 23 (middle)

Crabtree Publishing Company
www.crabtreebooks.com   1-800-387-7650

PMB 16A
350 Fifth Avenue
Suite 3308
New York, NY
10118

612 Welland Avenue
St. Catharines
Ontario
Canada
L2M 5V6

73 Lime Walk
Headington
Oxford
OX3 7AD
United Kingdom

Cataloging-in-Publication Data
Bishop, Amanda.
  Life in a pueblo / Amanda Bishop & Bobbie Kalman.
    p. cm. -- (The Native nations of North America series)
Includes index.
This book introduces children to the traditional daily life of the
Pueblo Peoples of the Southwest region prior to European
contact.
  ISBN 0-7787-0375-4 (RLB) -- ISBN 0-7787-0467-X (pbk.)
  1. Pueblos--Juvenile literature. 2. Pueblo Indians--Dwellings--
Juvenile literature. I. Bishop, Amanda. II. Title. III. Series.
  E99.P9K34 2003
  j978.9'004974

20039010031
LC

Contents

The Pueblo peoples

The word "pueblo" refers to the buildings and the villages of the Pueblo peoples.

The Native peoples of the **pueblos** have lived in the Southwest region of what is now the United States for hundreds of years. Their traditional home is in the **Four Corners** region of the Southwest—the area where the borders of present-day Arizona, New Mexico, Utah, and Colorado meet. When Spanish explorers came to the Southwest in the 1500s, they were amazed to see Native peoples living in apartment-style dwellings that housed many families. The Spaniards called the buildings pueblos. "Pueblo" means "village." The people who lived in the pueblos became known as the Pueblo peoples. They did not all live in one place or speak a single language, but their cultures had many common features.

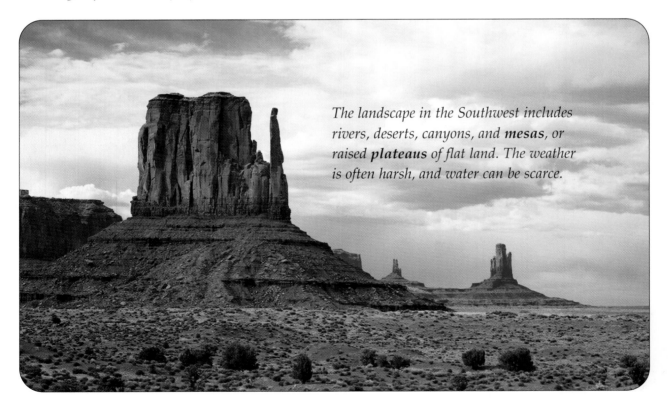

*The landscape in the Southwest includes rivers, deserts, canyons, and **mesas**, or raised **plateaus** of flat land. The weather is often harsh, and water can be scarce.*

Ancient relations

The Pueblo peoples are descendants of two ancient groups, most often called the Mogollon and the Anasazi. These cultures were among the first inhabitants of the Southwest. They lived in the region for nearly one thousand years. At first, they lived in **pithouses**, which were dug out of the ground. They survived by hunting and gathering wild foods. Eventually, both groups began to farm and to construct large stone dwellings— the first pueblos, as shown above.

Distinct cultures

During the 1300s, the ancient cultures abandoned the first pueblos. They split into several smaller groups and spread out, moving to areas along the river known as the Rio Grande and on the plateaus and mesas of Arizona and New Mexico. Each group developed a distinct lifestyle, culture, and language. The Pueblo peoples are described in this book as they lived when Spanish explorers first arrived. The Pueblo peoples of today continue to live in the Southwest and carry on many of the traditions of their ancestors.

Different lives and languages

All Pueblo peoples lived sedentary lifestyles, which means they stayed in one place year-round. There were some important differences among the peoples, however. The most noticeable differences were between the peoples in the eastern part of the region, near the Rio Grande, and the Hopi and Zuni in the west. The farther apart the pueblos were located, the fewer similarities there were among their cultures. In the east, each group lived in a single village—sometimes in a single, giant pueblo. In the west, however, the Zuni and Hopi peoples had many villages, and there was more than one pueblo in each village.

Language groups

The Pueblo peoples spoke—and continue to speak—many languages. People who study the history of the Pueblo peoples often group them according to their **language family**. In the east, most Pueblo peoples spoke languages belonging to the Tanoan language family or the Keresan language. In the west, the Hopi and Zuni each spoke their own languages, which are not related to those of any other Pueblo peoples.

(above) These women are at the Taos pueblo, the easternmost of the Rio Grande pueblos. The Hopi villages were the westernmost pueblos.

6

Eastern language groups

The people of the Tanoan pueblo villages speak three languages—Tiwa, Tewa, and Towa. The people of Isleta (Tuei, Tue-i), Taos (Teotho, Tuah-Tah), Sandia (Na-Fiat), and Picuris (We-Lai) speak Tiwa. At the San Juan (O'Kang), Santa Clara (Ka-'P'-Geh, Kha-'po), San Ildelfonso (Po'sogeh, Po Woh Geh), Nambe, Tesuque (Tet-Sugeh), and Pojoaque (Po-joageh, Pos-suwae-geh) pueblos, people speak Tewa. Towa is spoken at Jemez (Hemish, Wala-towa). The Keresan language is spoken at the pueblos of Acoma (Ako-me), Cochiti (Ko-'Chits, Katyete), Laguna (Ka-waik, Ka-waikah), San Felipe (Koots-Cha), Santa Ana (Tamaya), Santo Domingo (Khe-Wa), and Zia (Tsia).

Inside a pueblo

A pueblo was a dwelling with up to five floors. Each floor had several rooms, although the upper levels had fewer rooms than the lower levels had. The roofs of the lower rooms formed balconies for the upper rooms. Rooms along the outside of the pueblo had windows and doors that opened onto the balconies. These rooms were the living quarters, where people ate and slept. The inner rooms had no windows and were usually used for storage. On cold winter nights, however, people sometimes slept in the inner rooms.

Shut tight

Pueblos were very secure. Rooms on the ground floor usually had no windows or doors. People entered them through holes in the ceilings, which they reached by climbing a ladder onto the roof. The people of the pueblo pulled the ladders off the ground at night so that no one could enter without permission.

Building a pueblo

Pueblos were built by laying stones or **adobe** bricks on wooden frames. Adobe was a mixture of clay, straw, and water that became very hard when it dried. People shaped adobe into bricks, and they also used it to plaster the walls of pueblos. The plaster made the walls smooth and helped hold the bricks together. People often cut the wooden roof frames longer than the walls so that the ends would stick out. The ends of the frames were used as racks for hanging up clothing or food to dry.

People reached upper floors by climbing outdoor ladders from one level to the next. Members of a community often gathered on the rooftops of the pueblos to watch ceremonies or competitions.

8

Inside a family's quarters

In many pueblos, family members lived together in one room. There was little furniture except for benches along the walls. A fire pit kept the room warm and was occasionally used for cooking.

Cupboards were carved into the walls to hold containers such as baskets and clay pots. Family members made the pots and stored food, water, and other possessions in them. Clay jars were sometimes hung from the rafters in the ceiling.

There were many advantages to living in apartment-style dwellings. Neighbors could share supplies and help one another with jobs such as farming and pottery making.

Families, clans, and moieties

The Pueblo peoples have always placed great importance on family. In most pueblos, families lived together in one or two rooms. They worked together tending crops, housekeeping, creating handicrafts, and preparing food. The people of the pueblos also belonged to larger groups in their communities—**clans** or **moieties**. Clans were groups of related families. Moieties divided the people in a pueblo into two groups, regardless of family ties. The Hopi and Zuni were mainly grouped by clans, whereas the Tanoan people in the east followed a moiety system. The Keresan pueblos of the east grouped people into both clans and moieties.

A family rests after a day of gathering wild plums.

Moieties sometimes competed against one another in games such as this race.

Clans

Clans are made up of people who share the same ancestors. Among some pueblos, clans had many duties, whereas other pueblos had less formal clans. Western clans were **matrilineal**, which means children belonged to the clans of their mothers. Members of matrilineal clans usually lived near one another. When a woman got married, her husband came to live with her in or near her mother's home.

Moieties

The word "moiety" comes from a French word meaning "one half." In many eastern pueblos, people belonged to one of two moieties. The Summer People were responsible for village activities and ceremonies that took place during the summer months. The Winter People took over these responsibilities in winter. Moieties were often **patrilineal**—children belonged to their fathers' moieties.

Village life

Pueblo villages have always been based on a sense of community. Every person contributed to the success and well-being of the village as a whole. Traditionally, each village had one or more leaders. Some were elected by village members. Others were given their roles because of their families' positions within the village. The main leader was often called the village **chief**.

Moiety chiefs

Among the eastern pueblos, each moiety had a chief who led the pueblo while his moiety ran the village activities. In some Rio Grande pueblos, the two moiety chiefs answered to a third chief. The western pueblos usually did not have a single leader. Instead, they looked to the heads of the various clans for leadership. Some also had a village **council** that met to make decisions about village life. Most pueblos also had societies to which members of all clans and moieties could belong. They addressed concerns regarding medicine, hunting, and warfare.

Daily life

Pueblo leaders were responsible for protecting the villagers from harm, organizing social and political events, and ensuring that ceremonies and spiritual practices were properly performed. They were assisted by other officials who carried out their instructions. These officials organized work groups for such tasks as planting and harvesting crops, building and repairing pueblos, and performing important ceremonies. These work groups were made up of all the villagers, who followed the instructions of the officials.

Learning by watching and doing

The children of the Pueblo peoples spent much of their time with adults. Among the western pueblos, children were members of their clans from the day they were born. In the eastern pueblos, children became members of their moieties between the ages of six and twelve. Among all the pueblos, many parents also chose to pledge their children to a **society**, such as a hunting or healing society, at a young age. When the children grew up, they became active members.

Children learned a great deal from the adults of their pueblos. Mothers, sisters, and aunts often taught young girls the arts of pottery and basket making. Girls also learned how to sew and work with adobe so they could help with the maintenance of their pueblos. Fathers, brothers, and uncles showed young boys how to hunt, make tools and weapons, and participate in ceremonies. In the picture above, the young boy is learning how to make a bow and arrow used for hunting.

Sharing jobs

Men and women shared tasks such as farming, gathering plants, and weaving cloth. Boys and girls learned about their responsibilities and helped with the work when they could. Young children scared away crows from the fields and assisted their parents with household jobs such as preparing food, as shown below. Older members of a village told stories. Telling stories was a way for the Pueblo peoples to record their history. Stories were passed from one generation to the next, and they continue to be told today.

Fun and games

There was plenty of work to be done in a pueblo, but children and adults always found time for fun and games, too. Competitive races were often held. Games with canes or sticks were popular and were often accompanied by singing and drumming. People enjoyed playing string games by using their fingers to make shapes with loops of string. Boys and girls made toy pots, drums, whistles, dolls, and clay figurines to entertain themselves and to practice craft-making skills.

Farming

The Pueblo peoples were farmers, just as their ancient ancestors were. At first, all the Pueblo groups farmed in the same way. Men and women used digging sticks to till the soil, wooden shovels to dig trenches, and stone axes to clear land. They carried dirt, seeds, and plants in woven baskets. They were **flood farmers** who relied on floods caused by heavy rainfalls or melting snow to water their crops. Over time, however, peoples along the Rio Grande developed a new way of farming.

Mats could be lowered into the canals to direct the flow of the water among the crops.

Farming on the Rio Grande

Farmers along the Rio Grande learned to **irrigate**, or water, their fields by directing water from the river to their fields through ditches and canals. Irrigation allowed them to grow plants in more areas than flood farming did, which meant they could grow more crops. Farmers who used irrigation had to plant their crops on land that was located lower than the river. They dug a system of ditches and **canals** to direct water from the Rio Grande and the small streams and rivers near it to their farms. The water in the canals and ditches flowed downhill to the farmland below. Farmers used mats woven from plant fibers to direct the water through the system of canals. Although farmers and their families were responsible for raising their own crops, the responsibility for digging and maintaining the canals and ditches was shared by everyone in the village.

Irrigation depends on gravity to pull water downhill.

Farming in the west

Western Pueblo peoples used farming methods similar to those of the ancient cultures. Since there was no river nearby to use for irrigation, farmers grew crops only during the summer months, when rain often caused flash floods. Farming at these pueblos was less of a group activity than it was along the Rio Grande. Families farmed near their pueblos. They were careful to choose plots of land that received just the right amount of rain during the summer to water the plants. If the land was flooded by too much water or if the water picked up a lot of sand and mud as it traveled over the land, the plants would be washed away or buried. There were so many dangers to crops that many families planted on two or three different plots. If one plot was ruined, they might still have a successful harvest on the others.

Harvest time!

The Pueblo peoples relied on farming for three key crops: beans, squash, and **maize**, or corn. These staple foods made up much of their diet. Other crops included cotton, tobacco, and melons. Successful harvests provided enough food for the village, as well as **surplus**, or extra, food. The surplus was traded for other goods or was dried and stored for winter, when no crops grew.

Hunting and gathering

Farming provided the Pueblo peoples with maize, beans, and squash, but their diet included many more foods. Hunters tracked animals for meat. Gatherers scoured the landscape looking for nutritious plant foods. Hunting and gathering supplied the Pueblo peoples with food as well as with natural materials such as plant fibers and animal hides, bones, and feathers. For more on how people used these materials, see pages 22-25.

Hunting

A lot of wild animals lived on the lands surrounding the pueblos, but hunters were careful to catch only as many as they needed. Hunters often worked alone, but some pueblos organized groups to hunt for large animals such as antelope and deer. Some hunting groups traveled north to the Great Plains to hunt buffalo. Smaller animals such as rabbits, badgers, beavers, and rodents also provided meat and fur. To catch rabbits, large groups of men, women, and children helped the hunters by frightening the animals out of their burrows or by surrounding them in a circle.

Gathering

Pueblo peoples enjoyed the fruits of giant saguaro cactuses and agave, piñon, juniper, and plum trees. They also gathered nourishing roots, flavorful berries, acorns, and wild chilies. They ate seeds and made some, such as sunflower seeds, into oil. Wild plant foods were not always easy to find in the dry landscape surrounding the pueblos, but the people who gathered them knew where and when to find these essential plants.

Animals in the pueblo

Hunters captured eagles and hawks and raised them—not for food but rather for their feathers, which were used in ceremonies. At some pueblos, the eagles were allowed to **scavenge**, or find and eat, food scraps and to hunt for rodents such as mice. These birds helped keep the village clean. Many pueblos were also home to **domestic**, or pet, dogs and turkeys. Dogs were hunting companions. Turkeys were raised for their feathers.

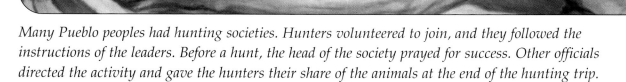

Many Pueblo peoples had hunting societies. Hunters volunteered to join, and they followed the instructions of the leaders. Before a hunt, the head of the society prayed for success. Other officials directed the activity and gave the hunters their share of the animals at the end of the hunting trip.

Preparing and cooking food

Preparing foods for cooking and storage was an important part of pueblo life. People had to cut the meat from hunted animals and clean the bones. Crops and wild plants had to be gathered and carried home. Many foods were dried or smoked so they could be stored and used later. Dried corn, beans, and wild nuts were often ground into **meal**, or coarse powder, which was used to cook many dishes. Although most pueblo rooms had a fire pit, people usually cooked outdoors. They cooked over open fires or in pits dug into the ground. The pits were heated with fire or hot rocks before food was placed in them. The food was then covered with ash and left to cook. In later years, many Pueblo peoples began using "beehive ovens," which were introduced by Spanish explorers. These dome-shaped ovens were often used to bake bread.

A young girl helped prepare bread dough, which her older sister is putting into a beehive oven to bake.

Mano and metate

The **mano** and **metate** were used to pound corn and other plant foods into meal. The metate was a flat or slightly indented stone on which kernels or seeds were placed. The mano was a smaller stone that was rubbed across the metate, back and forth or in circles, to crush the seeds. Dried meat was often ground together with seeds, nuts, or corn kernels.

Among the Hopi, a thin cornmeal bread called piki is still a favorite. Above, a Hopi girl is cooking it on a flat stone held over a fire by four rocks.

Making crafts

The Pueblo peoples used natural materials to make everything they needed. They collected plants and clay and used them to make household goods such as baskets and pottery.

Natural materials such as bone, shells, and stone were also used to make jewelry and decorations.

Baskets of all shapes and sizes were fashioned out of the grass, roots, bark, and leaves of many plants. The fibers were braided or woven together, and some were also attached to stiff wooden rims. The most secure baskets were made of tightly woven coils stitched together with thread made of **yucca** fiber. This type of basket could hold water without leaking! Other baskets were used for storing and carrying all kinds of goods.

Pottery

Clay pottery items, such as pitchers, bowls, and jugs, were ideal for food preparation because their surfaces heated quickly and kept food warm. To make these items, potters dug clay out of nearby clay pits. The moist clay was mixed with sand to thicken it. When the clay was ready, a potter shaped it by hand. The most common method involved layering long strips of clay on top of one another. When the shape was complete, the potter smoothed the surfaces using a polishing stone or a **gourd** such as a squash. He or she then dried and hardened the object in a fire or under the hot sun. Once the piece was dry, the potter decorated it using paintbrushes made of yucca leaves and **pigments** from local plants or minerals. The people of each region used their own patterns and colors. For example, Hopi pottery was often painted black and yellow and decorated with bird images.

Jewelry

The Pueblo peoples are known for making beautiful jewelry from bones, shells, and stones such as **turquoise**. Necklaces strung with hundreds of hand-shaped beads and ornaments carved from bones and shells were common. In later years, Europeans introduced metals such as silver to the Pueblo peoples. The Pueblo artisans began to combine the turquoise stones with silver, as shown right.

Clothing

Most Pueblo peoples wore clothing made of cotton fabric. People made the fabric by hand, using fibers they harvested from the cotton plants they grew. They cleaned the fibers and then spun them into thread using a **spindle stick and whorl**. The cotton thread was then woven into fabric on looms such as the one below. The natural color of the cotton fibers was off-white, but people used vegetable dyes to tint the thread or the finished cloth shades of green, orange, red, black, or yellow.

Using colored threads, weavers worked intricate designs into the fabric. People saved the brightest threads and finest cloths to make clothing for ceremonies. In addition to wearing fine clothing on special occasions, Pueblo peoples also wore ornamental beads and bracelets made of natural materials such as bone, shell, and turquoise. Feathers also adorned these special outfits. Pueblo people today dress in similar garments and ornaments on holidays and other special occasions.

Men's and boys' clothing

Pueblo peoples lived in one place through all the seasons, so they had to dress for all types of weather. On warm days, men wore **breechcloths** or **aprons**. A breechcloth was a rectangular piece of cotton that went between the legs and was secured with a belt. The edges of the cloth hung over the belt. An apron was made of cotton or other woven plant fibers, and was worn about the waist in the front and back. In cool weather, men wore **kilts**, or skirts. Pueblo men also clothed themselves in deerskin shirts and knee-length cotton leggings when the weather turned cold. Boys' clothing was very similar to that worn by the men.

Women's and girls' clothing

Throughout the year, women and girls wore **mantas**, or dresses, made of large rectangles of cotton. The ends of the fabric were fastened over one shoulder, leaving the other shoulder bare. A cotton sash was wrapped around the waist several times to belt the dress. In extreme heat, women and girls wore only fringed aprons around their waists similar to those worn by men and boys. In cold weather, people wore robes and blankets made of turkey feathers attached to netting. Infants and very young children were bundled in rabbit-skin robes to keep warm.

Heavier clothing made of rabbit, buffalo, and deer skin was stitched together with yucca-fiber string.

Footwear

On their feet, Pueblo peoples wore hard-bottomed sandals. To make these sandals, people braided strips of yucca leaves together in diagonal patterns. Cords made of yucca plant fibers were fastened around the sides of the sandals. Yucca fibers and turkey feathers could be entwined to form socks, which were worn with sandals in cool weather. Turkey feathers or tanned deerskin were also used to make warm **moccasins** for winter wear.

The Pueblo peoples crafted sandals that were shaped for the left and right feet.

Beliefs, rituals, and ceremonies

The spiritual beliefs of the Pueblo peoples have changed very little over time. The people continue to make their beliefs a part of their everyday lives. One of their most important beliefs is that each person must follow an honest, respectful "life road" or "life way" in order to ensure a long and happy life for themselves and the others in their pueblo. The different Pueblo groups honor many gods or **kachinas**, or ancestor spirits, and ask them for guidance and protection. Priests and **shamans**, or medicine men, instruct village members on rituals and ceremonies. Ceremonies vary from one pueblo to the next. People perform them to ask for rain or healing, and to offer thanks. Among some Pueblo groups, dancers wear masks to honor the kachinas. In other groups, dancers wear costumes but do not wear masks. The dancers move as a group. Men stomp their feet to a beat, and women shuffle their feet, always staying in contact with the earth below them. Some dancers also make hand gestures to imitate rainfall or growing crops.

Kachinas

Kachinas are asked to communicate with the gods on behalf of people. It is believed that these spirits live underground for one half of the year and among the people of the village during the other half. Kachinas often resemble animals, although some are named for a sound they make or for a human feature such as a long beard. Small figurines of kachinas, shown right, represent the kachina spirits and are given to children.

Kivas

Most pueblos have at least one **kiva**. The kiva is a ceremonial structure, often built underground. People enter it through a hole in the ceiling. A tall ladder leads from the ceiling to the floor. Sacred objects are stored in the kiva, and sacred rituals are performed there. Some kivas have an opening in the floor to represent the place where the first Pueblo people emerged from the underworld, as described in the **creation stories**. The stories tell that the earliest ancestors of the Pueblo peoples of today escaped from the underworld through a hole in its ceiling and then traveled to the spots where the first pueblos were built.

Trading goods

The Pueblo peoples were never alone in the Southwest. In the western part of the region, hunting-and-gathering peoples such as the Yavapai, Walapai, and Havasupai occasionally traded with the Pueblo nations. When the Navajo and Apache arrived in the region around the year 1400, they established trade relations with the Pueblo peoples. Plains nations from the north also traded with the northernmost Pueblos, such as the Taos. Nations traded with one another for clothing, plants, seeds, jewelry, pottery, baskets, and the raw materials used to make such objects.

Free to farm

Trade had several advantages for the Pueblo peoples. When other groups visited with meat, buffalo skins, deer hides, and other products, the Pueblo peoples could trade for those items rather than hunting themselves. Trading for goods allowed them to spend more time tending their crops, which meant they could have larger harvests and more foods to trade.

Tobacco and cotton

Most Pueblo peoples raised cotton and tobacco, which were valuable trade items. Tobacco was used for medicine and ceremonies by most nations in the area. The Pueblo peoples wove cotton fibers into cloth and clothing, which were desired items among the neighboring Navajo and Apache. The Navajo not only acquired woven cotton from the Pueblo peoples but also learned how to weave it. Soon the Navajo themselves traded woven fabric and products such as blankets, rugs, and clothing with the Pueblo peoples.

A band of Jicarilla Apache have set up camp near the Pecos pueblo. The people of the pueblo trade pottery and fabric for hides, bones, and moccasins.

Changing times, changing lives

The first Europeans to meet the Pueblo peoples were Spanish explorers. At first, the Pueblo groups treated the newcomers as guests but, before long, the Spanish explorers and **missionaries** took charge. They forced the Pueblo peoples to answer to Spanish authorities and demanded that they provide the Spanish settlers with work and goods. Missionaries established Roman Catholic churches and tried to **convert** the Pueblo peoples, or convince them to change their religious beliefs. If the people refused, they were often punished. Pueblo peoples were also forced to give up their own work to construct **missions**, or churches. The missionaries attacked spiritual beliefs, banned ceremonies, and destroyed religious objects. Many Pueblo peoples continued to practice their faiths in private, however. They combined their own beliefs with Christian beliefs.

The Pueblo peoples today

Since the Spaniards arrived in the 16th century, many outsiders have tried to change the ways of the Pueblo peoples. Despite their efforts, Pueblo culture has survived. Nineteen pueblo villages still exist in the Southwest, where Native people continue to live, work, and celebrate their heritage. Many of these villages welcome visitors. Some hold markets where Native artists display and sell their work. Many ancient sites that were inhabited by the ancestors of the Pueblo peoples are also open to visitors. If you would like to learn more about Pueblo peoples today, Pueblo history, or opportunities to see pueblos firsthand, try some of these web sites:

- www.indianpueblo.org
- www.puebloindian.com
- http://hewit.unco.edu/dohist/
  puebloan/start.htm

31

Glossary

Note: Boldfaced terms that are defined in the text may not appear in the glossary

adobe A mixture of clay, straw, and water used in the construction of pueblos

canal An artificial waterway

clan An extended family group

council An official group made up of village leaders who met to discuss important issues

flood farmer A farmer who relies on floods of water, such as heavy rainfall, to water crops

Four Corners The name given to the region of the Southwest where the borders of four present-day American states meet at one point

gourd A fleshy fruit with a hard outer layer

irrigate To direct water through ditches and canals from a water source to a crop field

language family A group of languages that have similar features or origins

mesa A raised, flat table of land

missionary A person who travels from place to place to convert people to a different faith

moccasins Shoes made of animal hides styled to cover the entire foot

moiety A group of one-half of a pueblo's dwellers that was responsible for running the pueblo during half the year

origin myth A story that describes the beginnings of a culture

pigment A natural coloring agent, such as red ochre

pithouse A dwelling of the ancient Southwest cultures that was dug out of the ground and covered by mats

plateau A flat table of land

pueblo An apartment-style structure made of stone or adobe bricks; a village of the Pueblo peoples

sedentary Describing a lifestyle that involves living in a permanent settlement year-round

society A group in a Pueblo community that was responsible for an aspect of daily life, such as hunting or healing

spindle stick and whorl A wooden rod and disc that was used to spin thread

yucca A plant that was often harvested for craft making

Index

1 2 3 4 5 6 7 8 9 0 Printed in the U.S.A. 2 1 0 9 8 7 6 5 4 3